S0-FGA-044

A Mashal & A Message

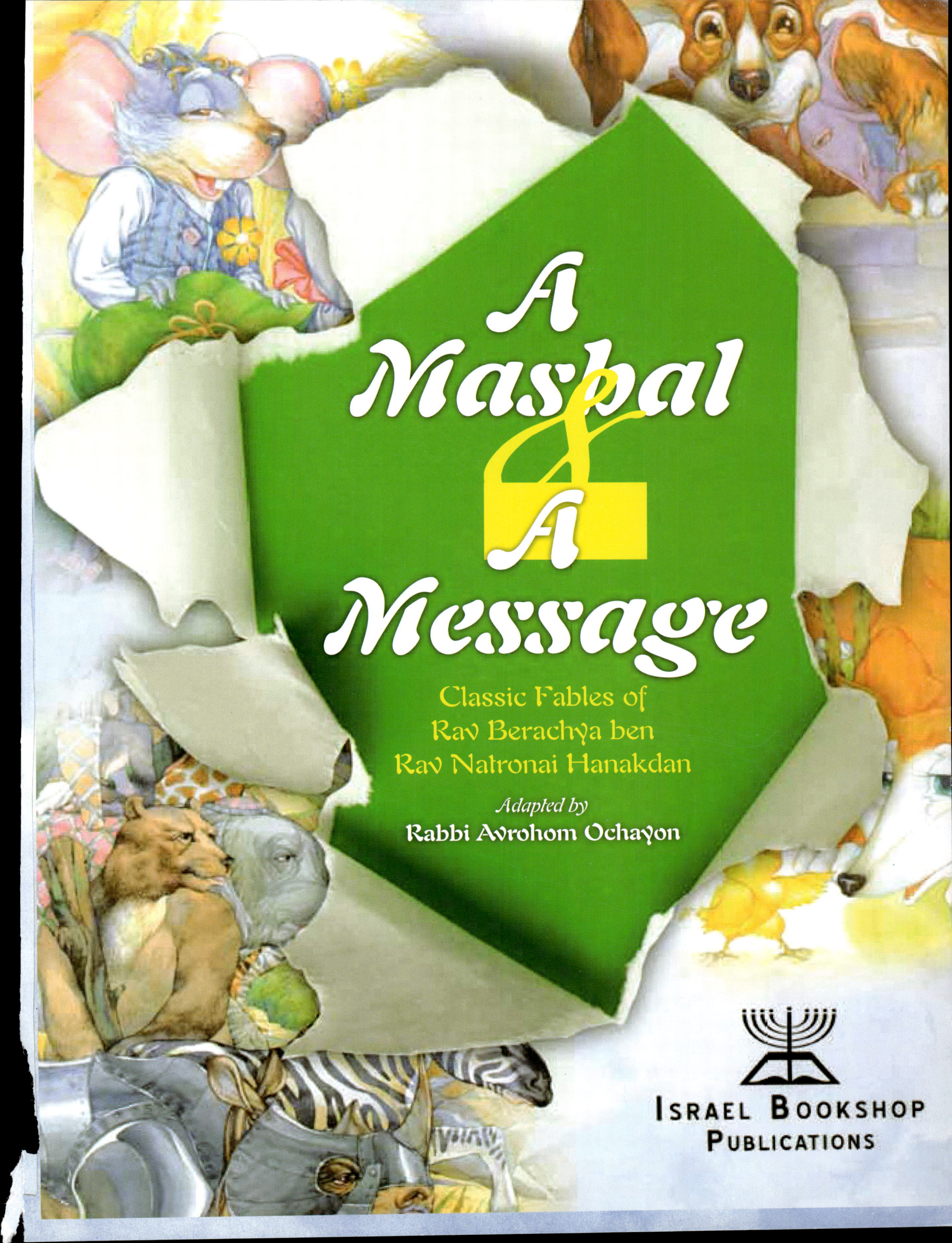

Classic Fables of
Rav Berachya ben
Rav Natronai Hanakdan

Adapted by
Rabbi Avrohom Ochayon

ISRAEL BOOKSHOP
PUBLICATIONS

Copyright © 2012 by Rabbi Avrohom Ochayon

ISBN 978-1-60091-220-7

All rights reserved. No part of this book may be reproduced or transmitted in any form or by any means (electronic, photocopying, recording or otherwise) without prior permission of the copyright holder or distributor.

Distributed by:
Israel Bookshop Publications
501 Prospect Street
Lakewood, NJ 08701

Tel: (732) 901-3009
Fax: (732) 901-4012
www.israelbookshoppublications.com
info@israelbookshoppublications.com

Printed in Israel

Distributed in Israel by:
Shanky's
Petach Tikva 16
Jerusalem
972-2-538-6936

Distributed in Europe by:
Lehmanns
Unit E Viking Industrial Park
Rolling Mill Road,
Jarrow , Tyne & Wear NE32 3DP
44-191-430-0333

Distributed in Australia by:
Gold's Book and Gift Company
3- 13 William Street
Balaclava 3183
613-9527-8775

Distributed in South Africa by:
Kollel Bookshop
Ivy Common
107 William Road, Norwood
Johannesburg 2192
27-11-728-1822

Introduction

A *mashal* is the quintessential tool in the hands of every *maggid*, teacher, and storyteller. Since the beginning of time, those who have wished to teach a lesson to others have taken advantage of this powerful medium. When the focus of an issue is on a fictional character rather than on the person himself, the person's defenses come down, and the lesson being taught is able to slip right in.

Rav Berachya ben Rav Natronai Hanakdan was a master of *meshalim* during the Middle Ages. Author of the sefer *Mishlei Shualim* ("Fox Fables"), he gathered over 100 fables, *meshalim* that contain significant messages within them. These *meshalim* are potent, and have been used effectively throughout the generations by those wishing to crystallize important Jewish themes and lessons.

The power of a *mashal* becomes even more apparent when it comes to children. Fables, especially, with foxes that are hungry, frogs that are jealous, and clever chickens and birds, are extremely popular with youngsters. When a child hears a story about a weak chick who comes up with a plan and outsmarts a wily (and of course hungry) fox, that truly drives home the message that intelligence and forethought are superior to physical strength. And the downfall of the traitorous bat, who turned against his friends in order to ensure that he remain on the winning side, speaks louder than words about the importance of loyalty.

In *A Mashal and a Message*, author Rabbi Avrohom Ochayon presents eleven of Rav Berachya ben Rav Natronai Hanakdan's wondrous fables—for children. Each *mashal*, or fable, has been age-appropriately adapted, and is told over in a most endearing and child-friendly way. The beautiful illustrations that accompany each page further enhance the power of the stories and their far-reaching lessons.

It is our hope that *A Mashal and a Message* accomplishes its intended goal, entertaining and providing enjoyment for your child—even as it teaches him some of life's most important lessons.

Table of Contents

7 The Greedy Dog

11 The Mouse and His Spouse

17 The Frog Who Pretended To Be a Doctor

21 The Donkey Who Wanted Attention

25 The Dog's Bell

29 The Chick Outsmarted the Fox

35 The Traitorous Bat

43 The Jealous Frog

49 The Bird's Trick

57 The Bull's Mistake

61 The Proud Cedar Tree and the Humble Bush

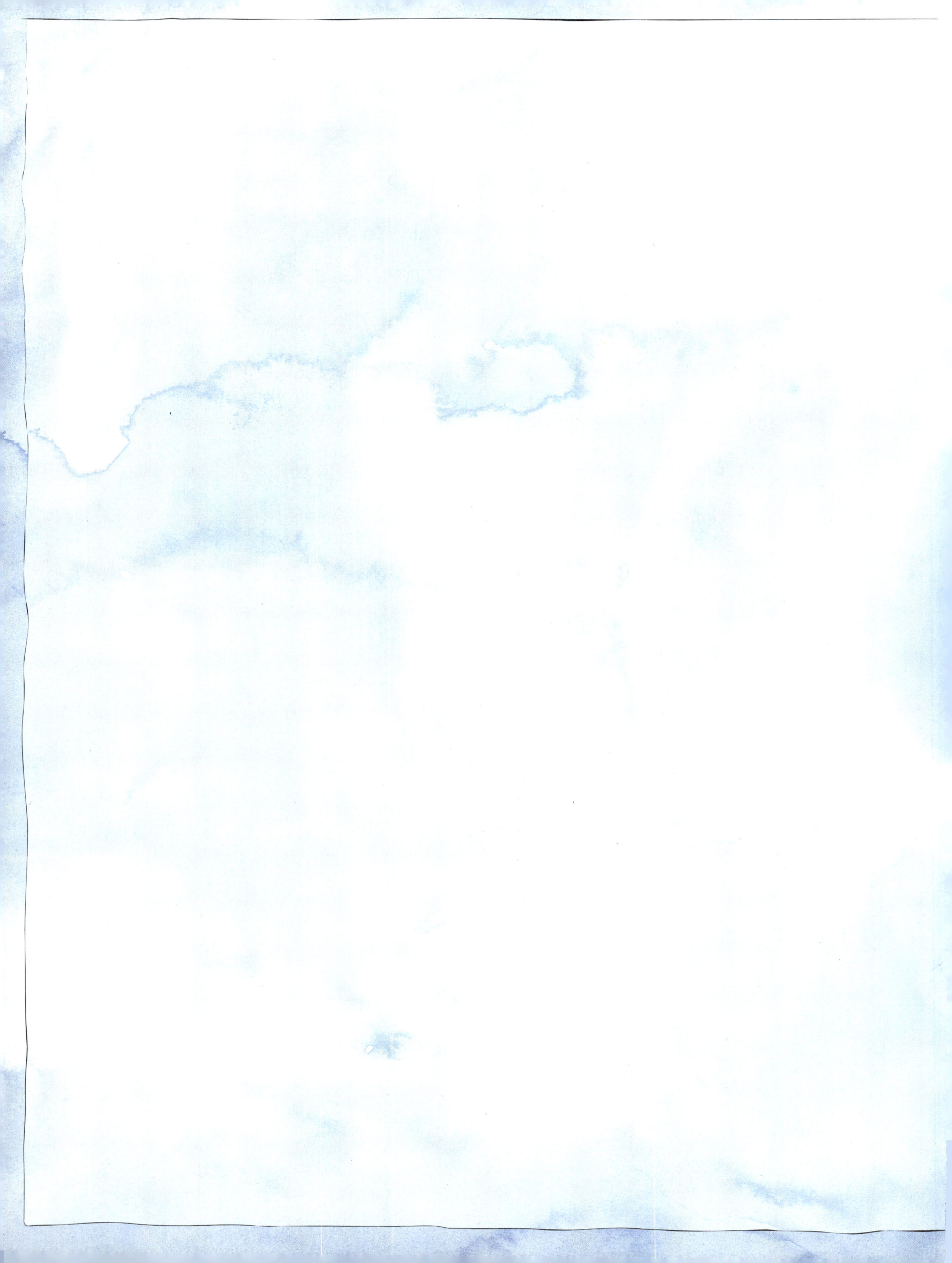

The Greedy Dog

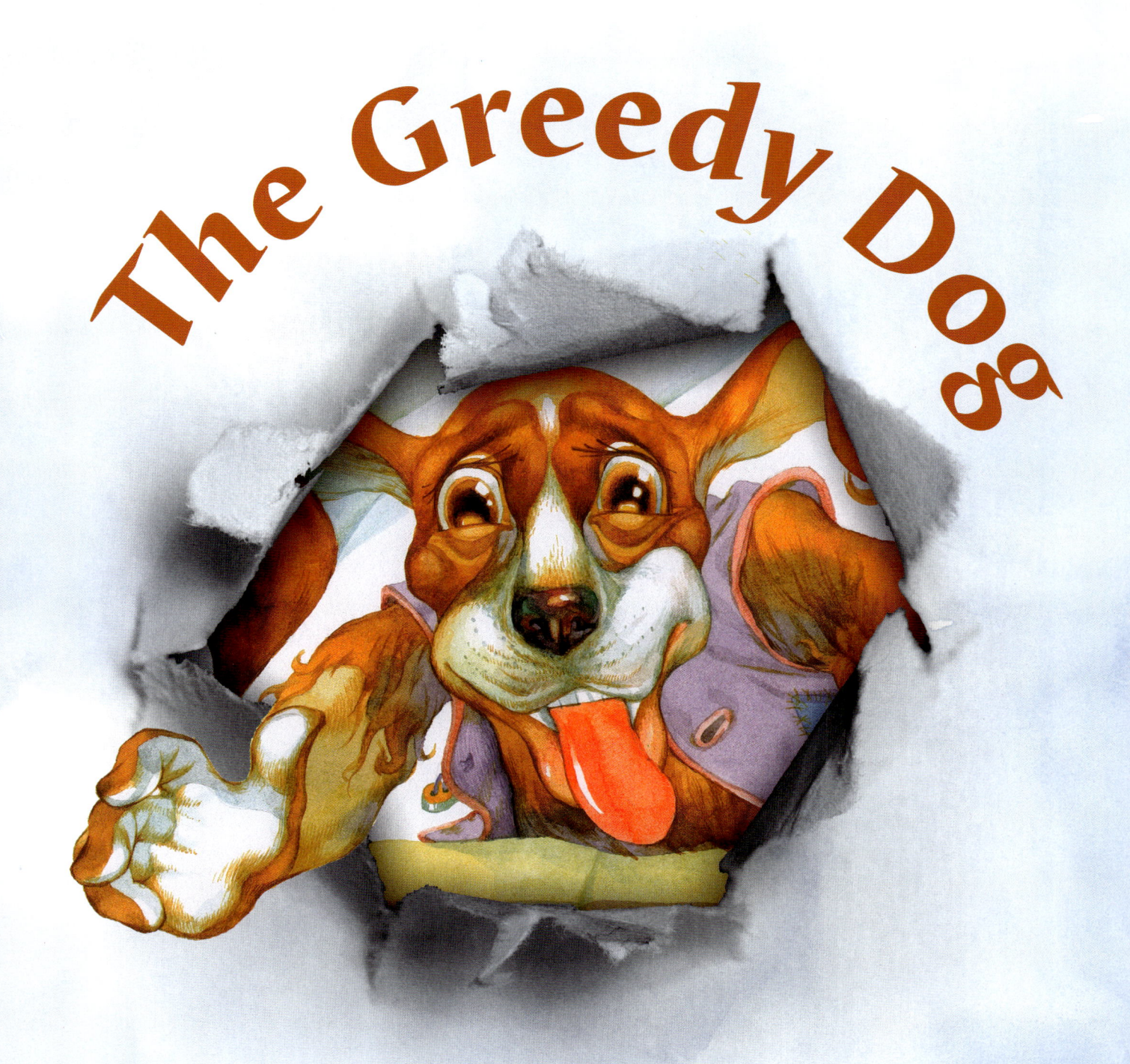

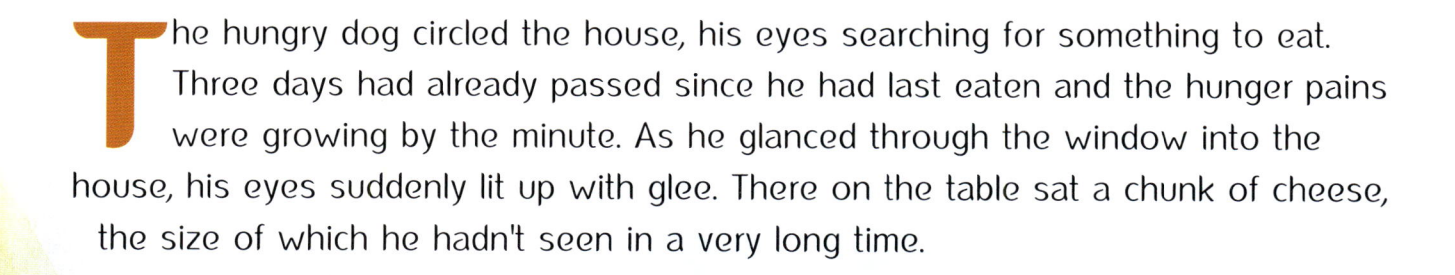

The hungry dog circled the house, his eyes searching for something to eat. Three days had already passed since he had last eaten and the hunger pains were growing by the minute. As he glanced through the window into the house, his eyes suddenly lit up with glee. There on the table sat a chunk of cheese, the size of which he hadn't seen in a very long time.

The dog quickly looked to the right and then to the left to see if anyone was watching. When he was sure that the house was empty, he jumped through the window, grabbed the cheese with his mouth and started running as fast as he could. The dog ran and ran as fast as his feet would carry him until he reached a stream far away from the house. "No one will see me here," he thought to himself, and he decided to take a rest by the water.

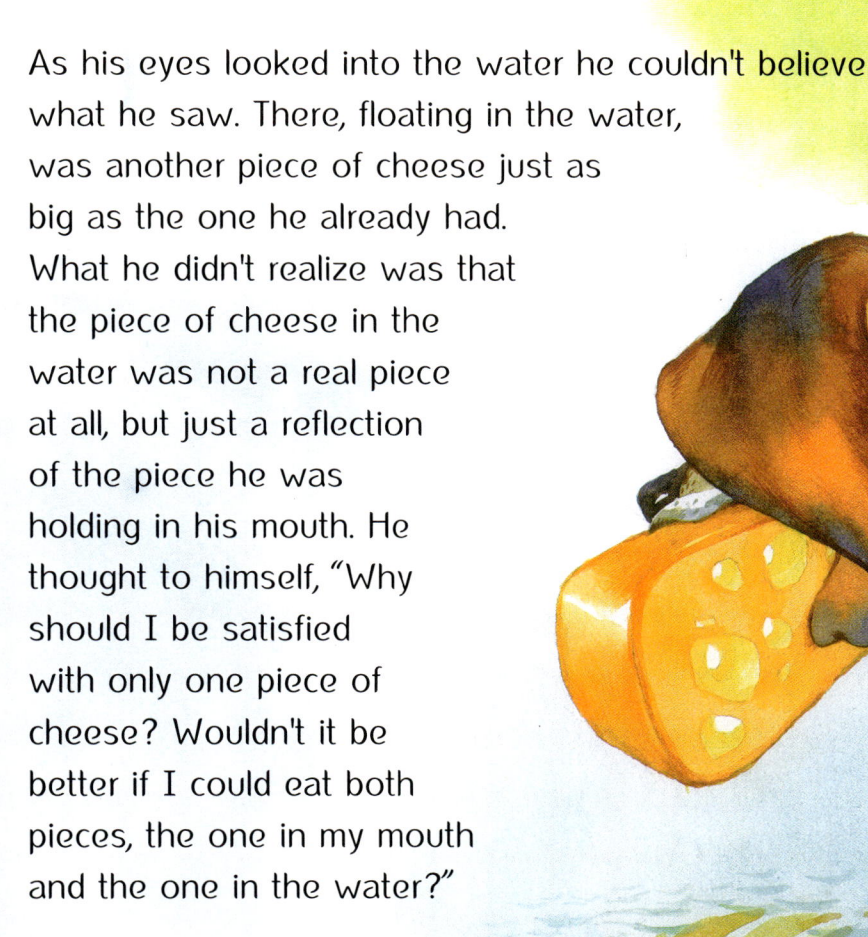

As his eyes looked into the water he couldn't **believe** what he saw. There, floating in the water, was another piece of cheese just as big as the one he already had. What he didn't realize was that the piece of cheese in the water was not a real piece at all, but just a reflection of the piece he was holding in his mouth. He thought to himself, "Why should I be satisfied with only one piece of cheese? Wouldn't it be better if I could eat both pieces, the one in my mouth and the one in the water?"

As the dog stuck his face into the water and opened his mouth wide to grab the second piece of cheese, something terrible happened. Can you guess what it was? The chunk of cheese in his mouth fell straight into the water and quickly disappeared, along with the second piece that was floating in the water.

"Oh, how foolish I was," he howled and growled.
"Because I wanted two pieces instead of one,
    I'm still as hungry as ever, for now I have none!"

WHAT IS THE LESSON?

If we always look for more and more,
Even what we have we will lose for sure!

The Mouse and His Spouse

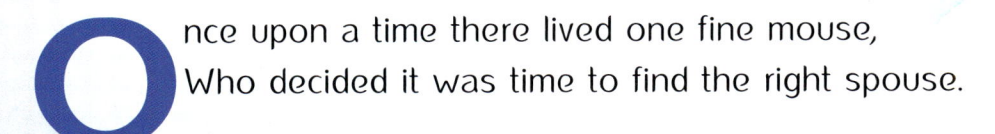

Once upon a time there lived one fine mouse,
Who decided it was time to find the right spouse.

"But," he thought to himself, "I will not be like the rest,
My wife must be the absolute best."

He first asked the sun, that big ball of fire,
"Will you please be my wife? It is you that I desire."

The sun answered back in a very sweet voice,
"I think you may have made a terrible choice.

"You
want
me for a
wife? I do not
know why,
For the clouds
certainly are much better than I.

"They cover me over when I'm shining so
bright,
Taking away from the world my heat and my light."

When the mouse heard these words he changed his decision,
And to the clouds up high he directed his vision.

He called out to them, politely and loud,
"Oh beautiful cloud, so respectful and proud,

"Will you please be my mate? It is you I wish to marry.
And in my heart, I promise, the greatest love for you I will carry."

But the clouds answered back to the mouse with a cry,
"We do not have any power in the sky!
"From east to west it is the wind that blows us around."
Then all of a sudden they were nowhere to be found.

14

The mouse didn't give up hope, he didn't despair,
He just took off his hat and declared to the air:

"My dear precious wind, will you please marry me?
For that you rule like a queen it is plain to see."

The wind said, "I'm sorry, but I cannot agree,
For there is something else much stronger than me."

"Tell me what it is," the mouse exclaimed in shock.
"It is the wall around the city," answered the wind, "solid as a rock."
The mouse ran over to the wall, oh, so strong,
And began to sing a most beautiful song.

"My dear mighty wall that no one can break,
It is you for a wife that I wish to take."

The wall then answered back with an angry shout,
"No one can break me? What are you talking about?

"Can't you see all of these holes made by you mice,
Making me look ridiculous, like I'm full of lice!"

The mouse looked around, he was really ashamed.
Then he sat on the ground, feeling tired and pained.

"A wife so extra special I was trying to find,
But now everyone has sent me back to my very own kind.

"It seems that for greatness which was not mine, I was searching,
While my true life I was plain and simply overlooking."

So off he went, back to the land of the mice,
And with pride and joy found a spouse ever so nice.

What is the lesson?

Every person must know his proper place. Whoever looks for honor in other places will find himself back where he started.

The Frog Who Pretended To Be a Doctor

From her spot where she sat in the swamp, the bored frog set her eyes on two bulls plowing a nearby field.

After watching them for several hours she decided to befriend them. When the bulls finished plowing the field and lay down in the shade to rest, the frog jumped in front of them and said, "My dear bulls, I would like to inform you that I am a professional doctor with a lot of experience. I have healed many animals, who now owe me their lives. I am always, always right!

"Would you like me to check you to see if you are sick?" she asked, full of hope, and waited for an answer.

But the bulls just kept quiet and twitched their tails. Then the older of the two opened his tired eyes and asked in a whisper, "Tell me, my proud frog, if you are really an experienced doctor, then why are your cheeks so green instead of being red? Why does your skin color look like the color of sick people who are dying? Do you not know how to even heal yourself?"

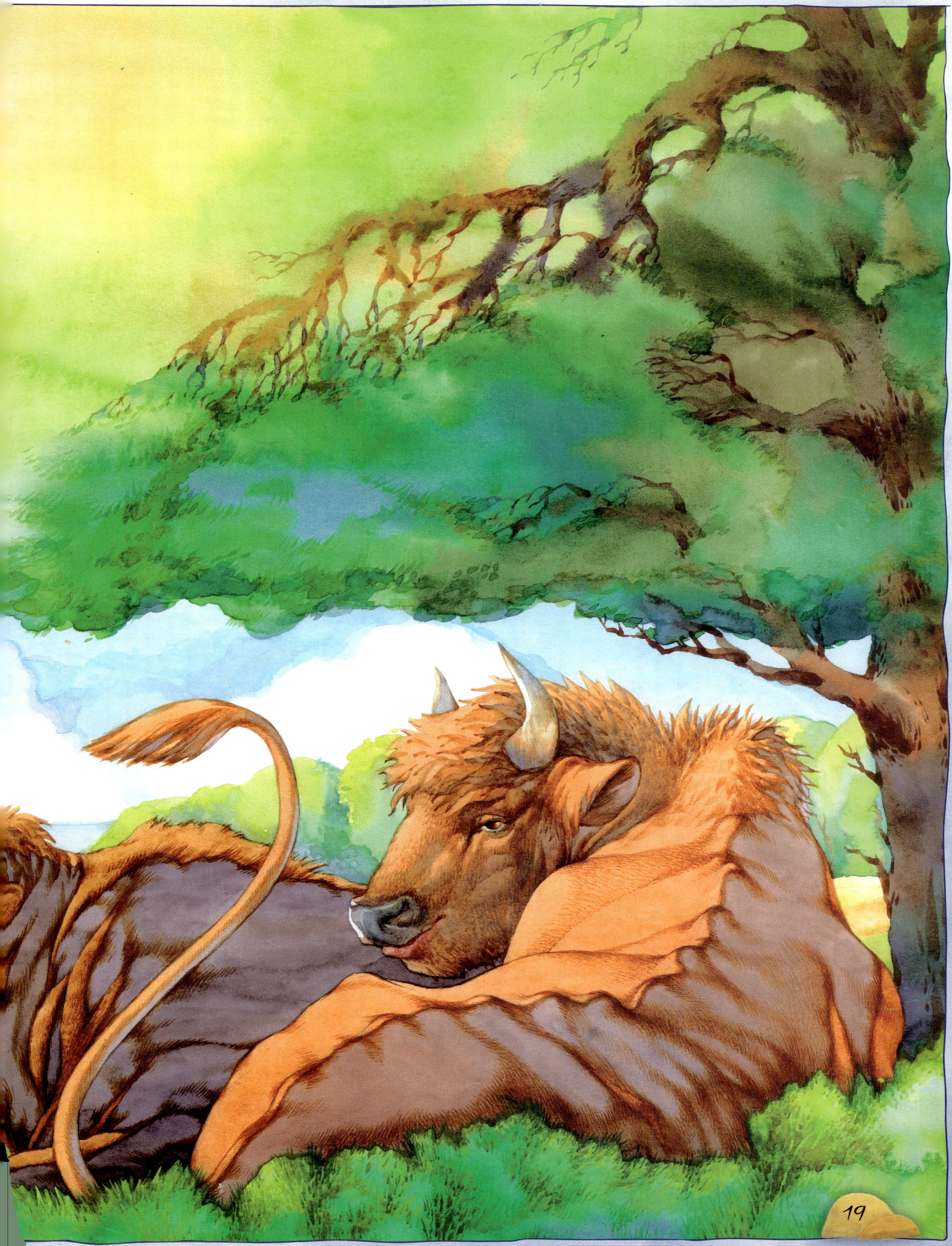

The frog realized that she was not successful in fooling the bulls. Embarrassed, she jumped back into the swamp and promised herself that she would never pretend to be a doctor again.

What is the lesson?

A person should never try to lie, because sometimes the lie becomes revealed and the liar is left feeling very embarrassed.

The Donkey

Who Wanted Attention

In the home of the honored prince,
There lived a cute little dog named Vince.

An object of joy he was for his master,
All day he would run around him, faster and faster.

Whenever the prince would enter the house,
Vince would jump on him like a playful mouse.

The prince spoiled the dog for he loved him so,
He would shower him with affection from head to toe.

The donkey quietly watched this from inside his stable,
His heart filled with

jealousy, to ignore it he
was not able.

"Why does the dog alone merit such
 attention,
Am I not deserving of even a mention?

"Perhaps if I behave the same as he,
I would get the same love directed at me."

That same day, when the prince returned from the
royal table,
The donkey hurried and
jumped out of his
place in the
stable.

On his back legs he stood proudly,
Then he faced his master and neighed loudly.

He placed his front hooves on the prince's shoulders to hold himself up,
And, with his super - long tongue, began to lick his face, just like a pup!

He expected his master to shriek from delight,
To give him a hug, and hold him tight.

But, instead, the prince screamed, "Save me from this crazy donkey who has gone mad!
Soon he will trample me with his feet! Oh my, will that be bad!"

As the sound of his screams reached every ear,
All of the people in the house jumped up to hear.

They picked up sticks and stones, one by one,
And came to save the prince, on the run.

They chased away the donkey with blow after blow,
And all their big stones at him they did throw.

As fast as he could, the donkey ran back to his stable,
Where to think about what happened he was finally able.

He realized that if one looks for honor which is not his own,
He will only end up feeling embarrassed and alone.

WHAT IS THE LESSON?

Everyone has their own good qualities to be proud of. Whoever tries to imitate someone else will usually end up losing, not gaining.

The Dog's Bell

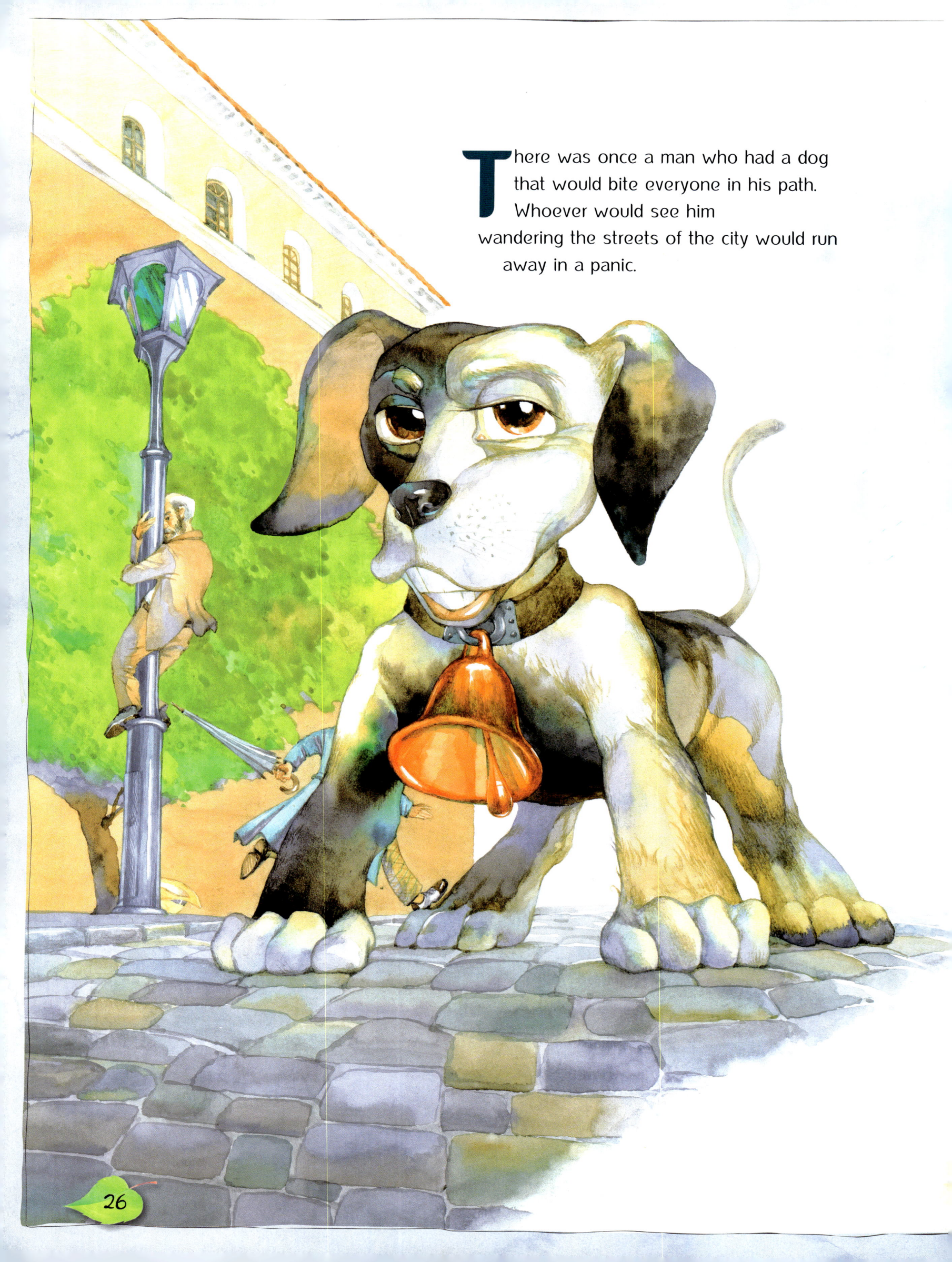

There was once a man who had a dog that would bite everyone in his path. Whoever would see him wandering the streets of the city would run away in a panic.

Everyone was afraid of getting bitten by the mischievous dog! Slowly but surely, the owner began receiving complaints from the townspeople. He was firmly asked to keep a better watch on his rebellious dog and to teach him that he must not harm the people in the town.

So what did the man do to solve this problem? He tied a metal chain around the dog's neck to which he attached a loud bell. So now, when the dog would walk around the town, the sound of the bell could be heard from far away: "Ding dong, ding dong." When the people would hear the ringing of the bell, they would quickly hide themselves from the bad dog.

The dog began to feel very proud of himself. "I am a very important and special dog, privileged and well respected. What other dog has a bell like mine? What other dog can be heard from so far away like me?"

The dog did not understand that

his owner had tied the chain around his neck in order to warn the townspeople of his presence. One day an old and wise dog grabbed hold of him and whispered into his ear: "Why do you feel so proud, my brother? Do you think that the chain around your neck with the bell is a sign of your importance or of your honor? No, no! Your master tied the chain around your neck because you are a mischievous dog, constantly biting the townspeople and causing fear to every passerby!"

What is the lesson?

An evil person who seems to get respect from those around him should know that those who honor him are only doing so to protect themselves from his evil ways, and not because they really value him.

The Chick Outsmarted the Fox

In a little town there once lived a rooster and a hen. They lived peacefully as husband and wife, and together they raised eight cute little chicks. One year, however, there was a big famine in that town. No rain fell from the sky and no wheat grew in the fields. The chickens soon became extremely hungry and their hearts filled with worry. One day the rooster turned to the hen and said, "My dear wife, why are we sitting in this town waiting to die of starvation? Let us go to the next town where my rich uncle lives. He has a barn full of fresh and delicious wheat that we could eat from."

The hen agreed with her husband's idea, and early the next morning, the two of them set out together with their eight little chicks for the neighboring town. They walked and walked all day long, barely even taking a rest, until finally at sunset they arrived at their uncle's house, where they received a warm and happy welcome.

The chicken family stayed with their uncle for three months, where they had plenty of wheat to eat and water to drink. When the harvesting season arrived the chicken turned to his wife and children and said, "The time has come to return home. The wheat has certainly grown again in the fields of our town, so we will no longer lack any food."

The chicken then announced, "Listen carefully, my children. We must each take a stalk of wheat in our mouths which we will carry back with us to our town. We will keep these stalks in our mouths until we are sure that the famine has ended. Only then will we throw these away and gather new ones in their place." Seven of the chicks took stalks in their mouths, but the eighth one was weak and ill and could hardly even walk. He didn't have enough strength to carry a stalk of wheat in his mouth, so he just followed behind his brothers ever so slowly.

The family of chickens arrived at the forest and began marching among the trees. "One, two, one, two," called out the father chicken with joy and then suddenly he stopped! A hungry and scary-looking fox had come out from between the branches and stood in front of the chicken family.

His eyes were mean and his mouth looked ready to swallow a good meal. The chicken froze in fear and did not know what to do. If he would try to run backwards, the fox would surely chase after him and devour him together with his whole family. But if he would continue marching forward, the fox would catch them one after the other.

While he was thinking, however, the fox walked over to the eighth little chick and began to speak to him. "What are those things in all of your brothers' mouths?" the fox asked in a sly voice. The chick quickly answered back in a very serious tone: "Those are the tails of all of the big foxes that my brothers killed."

The fox then asked, a little confused, "So why isn't there anything in your mouth?" The chick answered back with a stern voice, with his hands on his hips, "Ho, ho, that is because I have been waiting for you since early this morning! Please turn around so that I can tear off your tail and peel off your skin like my brothers did to your brothers!" When the fox heard these words, he became terrified. He turned right around and disappeared back into the forest, leaving the family of chickens to continue safely on their journey home.

What is the lesson?

In order to defeat a fox, one does not need to be strong. Just like the weak chick outsmarted the fox with his quick wit, so too, a person can defeat someone stronger than himself with intelligence and careful words.

The Traitorous Bat

36

The forest was in an uproar, it was quite a sight,
The animals and the birds were preparing for a fight.

A few days before, the decision had been made,
To decide on whose head the royal crown should be laid.

Would it be one of the animals, to rule from the ground?
Or maybe the eagle, the greatest bird to be found?

Opposite each other stood the two teams,
Filling the air with their shouts and their screams.

All were ready for the greatest of wars to begin,
Proudly, each thought that their side would win.

Waiting all alone, on a branch up high,
Sat the bat, who thought to himself with a sigh:

"On the one hand my body is like an animal, I guess,
On the other hand I'm like a bird with the wings I possess.

"What should I do? I dare not be wrong.
To which of these groups do I really belong?"

The bat thought, then thought some more,
Debating which side he'd join in this war.
Then a brilliant idea entered his head.
"I'll just wait and see by whom the battle will be led.

"If the animals are on top, it's them I will choose,
But if the birds are winning, I'll pick them, I cannot lose!"

With the rise of the sun, the trumpets were sounded,
The birds were attacked, the animals were pounded.

Not for a moment did either side take a rest,
They each took a beating, yet they gave it their best.

When afternoon arrived, it looked pretty clear,
The animals were winning, they were almost there.

So down came our friend from the place where he sat,
To fight alongside the bear and the cat.

He attacked all the birds with the strength of a horse,
One, then two more, without showing remorse.

But as evening approached, the tide seemed to turn,
The birds would be victorious, the bat would soon learn.

"Oh no," thought the bat, "I chose the wrong side,
I must switch to the birds, by their rules I
must abide."

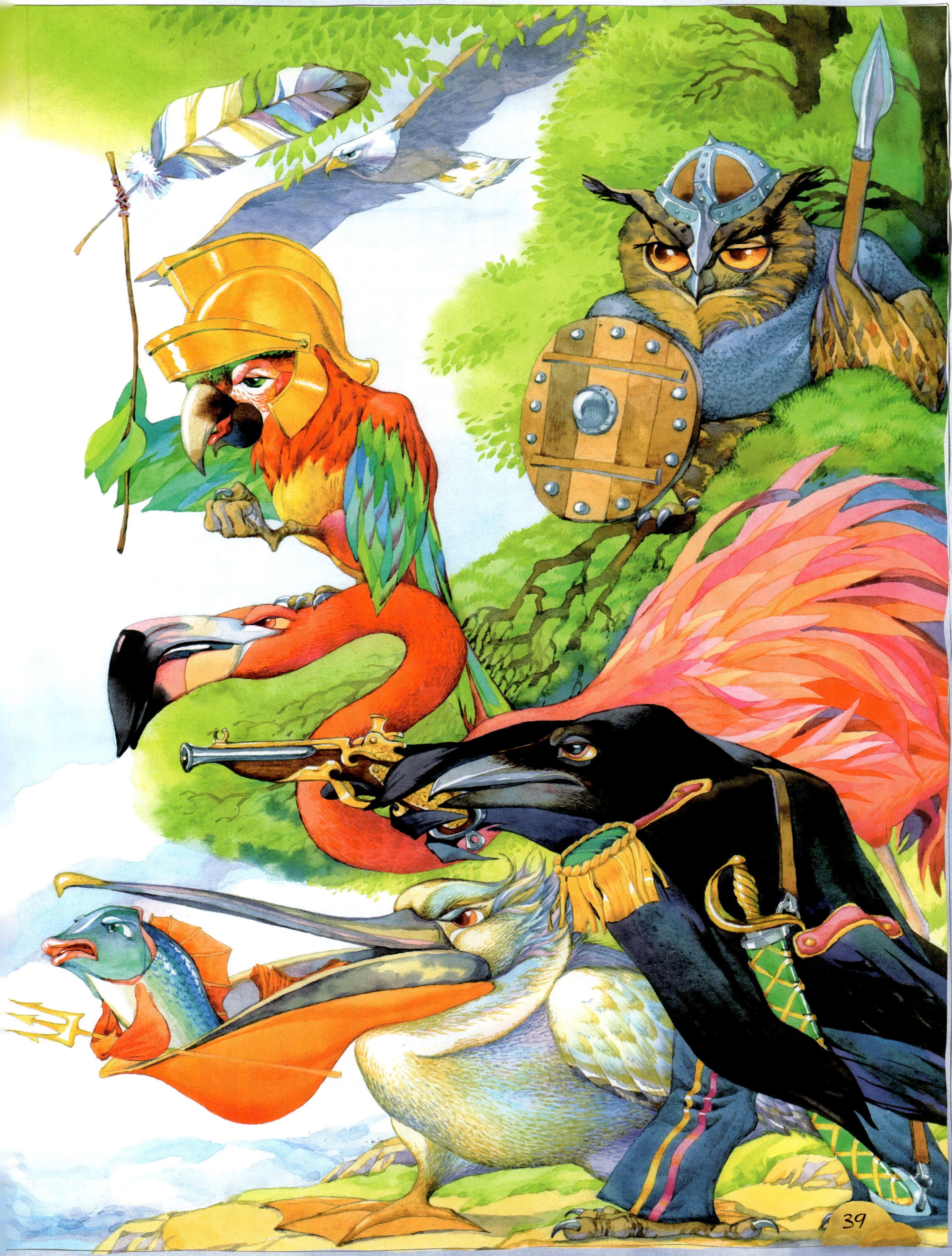

He spread out his wings and started to fight,
He struck at the animals with all of his might.
The birds, for their part, were not very glad.
"A traitor's among us," they called out, real mad.

"You fought with us bitterly, just a few hours ago,
And now you come to join us, to be our friend? Oh, no!"

As the dark of the night covered the forest so vast,
The birds claimed their victory, it was over at last.

The animals all bowed their heads with great awe,
Toward the eagle, with his crown, the new master of law.

But what should be done with the bat, that big traitor,
Who fought with the animals and tried to join the birds later?
The birds brought him for judgment to the eagle, their king,
To decide what punishment would be the right thing.

The Great Eagle thought hard and made up his mind,
"For looking the wrong way, you must become blind.

"The hair on your head we will cut off or shave,
And then you'll be sent to live alone in a cave."
The birds all gathered and the punishment was done.
Off to the cave, they sent the blind one.

What is the lesson?
If we turn from our values and betray
a dear friend,
All alone, like the bat, we will be left
in the end.

The Jealous Frog

At the doorway to the grinding mill there stood a mouse, whose hands were filled with wheat and flour. He was in a great mood and he felt like the richest creature in the world. He sang a happy tune while clapping his hands and stamping his feet to the rhythm of the beat.

Suddenly a frog arrived on the scene. When she saw that the mouse was so excited she asked him: "Why are you so merry, my dear mouse? What has made you so happy this morning?"

"How can I not be happy?" the mouse answered back. "When I am in the grinding mill I have so much food! There is wheat in every corner and flour is spread all over the floor. As soon as the grinder goes home, I come out of my hole, stretch out my hands and collect an endless supply of yummy food."

When the frog looked at the happy mouse, her heart filled with jealousy. She could not accept the fact that the mouse had more than her, so she started to think of ways to hurt the mouse. The jealous frog said: "My dear mouse, it is true that you have so much food available to you, but how great is your fear and worry! If the grinder would ever see you, he would run after you and hit you until you would die. If you would come with me to my home, you would see that I live in peace and nobody scares me. I don't have to come out of a hole in the middle of the night and I, too, have plenty of food."

"And where is your home?" asked the mouse with wide – open eyes. The frog answered in a soft voice, "Come with me for a walk and I will show you my home." They both started walking and when they got to the river the frog pointed her hand and said, "There, across the river, is my charming home, full of food, delicacies and all kinds of sweet things."

45

"How will I cross the river?" asked the mouse, who did not know how to swim. The frog took out a string from her pocket and tied it to her foot. "The other end of the string you will tie to your foot," she said, "and I will pull you through the river until we get to the other side. Then we will have a party together in my house."

The frog really didn't want to bring the mouse to her house at all. What she really planned to do was to drown the mouse in the river. The two began their marvelous journey and the frog dragged the mouse into the middle of the river.

Suddenly, an eagle burst forth from the sky, and from high above he saw the two of them in the river. "Here is an easy catch for me," thought the eagle and he smiled as he plunged quickly towards the river. He grabbed hold of the mouse with his beak and together with him he dragged the frog along too. He flew with them both to his nest, where he prepared to have a delicious meal. When the eagle looked at the skinny, hairy mouse, he decided not to eat him, and he let him go. However, the frog's soft and plump body made a very nice meal for the eagle.

When the mouse saw that he was free from the string, he quickly escaped back to the safety of his little hole.

What is the lesson?

Whoever tries to harm someone else will himself be punished.

The Bird's Trick

In the royal palace there was great joy. The king had presented his daughter with a special gift, a singing bird in an impressive round cage made out of gold. The princess took the beautiful cage and hung it on a hook in her room. The bird sang such wonderful melodies that the princess danced along as she listened. The bird seemed to be very happy, but in reality it was very sad for it wished to be free and flying high in the sky. The bird thought to itself, "I would rather be free than live in this golden cage. Even seeds from the garbage would be tastier to me than this royal palace food."

It happened one day that the bird saw one of the king's mighty soldiers preparing to set out on a long journey. The bird called out to him in a pleading voice. "Listen, please, mighty knight. You will be traveling across the ocean to the place where my cousin lives. If you happen to meet her, tell her about me. Tell her that I am trapped in a prison and that I long to be free. Please ask her for some advice that will help me escape my royal cage."

51

The knight nodded his head and took off his hat as a sign of understanding. "I will do as you requested, my beloved bird. If I meet your cousin I will ask her for advice." He mounted his horse with one easy jump and, galloping along, he and his horse disappeared into the horizon. After the knight and the horse sailed on a big ship, they finally arrived on the other side of the ocean. One day, as he was walking around in the faraway land, he suddenly saw the bird's cousin in a tree. "Birdy, birdy," called the knight and then he proceeded to tell her the sad story of the singing bird in the palace. The bird listened carefully to the knight's story and then, suddenly, she dropped onto the ground! The knight came close to her and picked her up. He sprinkled some cold water on her face and he tried to warm her up and revive her, but, painfully, he understood that she had died. He threw her onto the ground and prepared to leave, when to his surprise the dead bird started to move. She flew up high and disappeared among the clouds, leaving the knight completely bewildered.

When the knight returned to the royal palace, he hurried right away to the bird's cage in the princess's room. He told the bird the strange story of her cousin whom he had met on the other side of the ocean. The bird listened very carefully to what the knight was saying, and when he finished his story she thanked him from the depths of her heart. "Thank you very much, my mighty knight," she said, while in her mind she was already planning her escape.

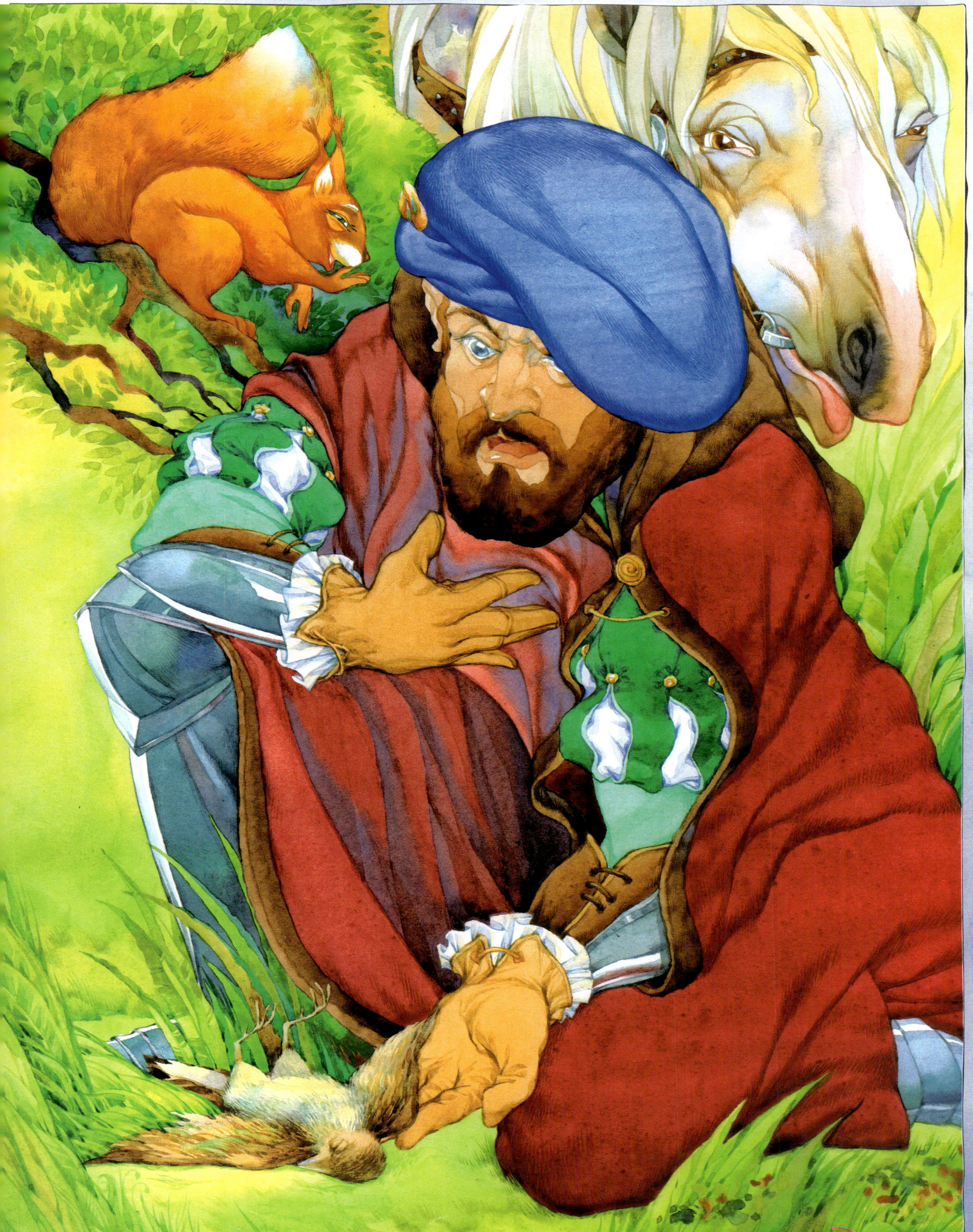

When the princess woke up the next morning, her ears were greeted by complete silence. "Why is the bird not singing this morning?" she called out in a fluster as she ran over to the golden cage. "Oh, my, oh, my!" the princess cried out in a panic, for the bird that she loved so much lay flat on the floor of the cage. Her wings didn't flap, her eyes didn't blink, her beak didn't move, she didn't even make a sound. The princess opened the cage and lifted up the bird very carefully. She sprinkled some water on her, she tried to warm her up with her hands, but nothing seemed to help. The beautiful singing bird appeared to be dead. The princess threw the bird out into the garden and then fell onto her bed, sobbing. "My bird has died!" she cried bitterly. "Whatever shall I do? This is absolutely terrible."

Just at that moment, her ears detected a strange sound. As it got louder and louder, it became very familiar and she recognized the sound. She quickly looked outside and, to her amazement, she saw her bird sitting on the branch of a nearby tree! The bird was singing with her beautiful voice, as if she had not been lying lifeless only moments ago. The princess understood that the bird had tricked her by pretending to be dead so that she would be able to escape from her cage. In truth, she was not dead, nor was she even sick. All she had wanted was to be free at last.

WHAT IS THE LESSON?

With the careful use of one's intelligence, even
tiny birds can think of an idea and outsmart
both a knight and a royal princess.

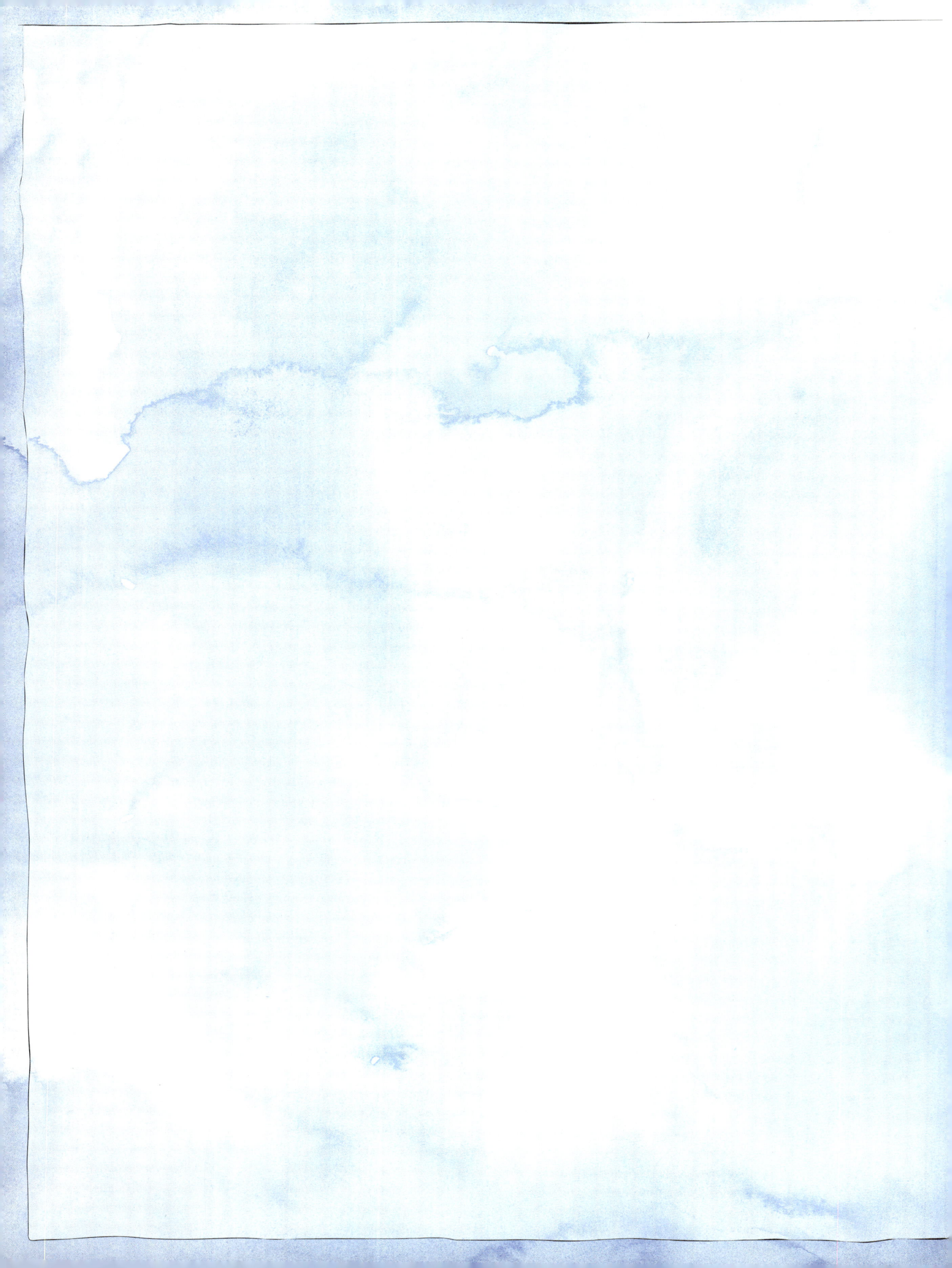

The Bull's Mistake

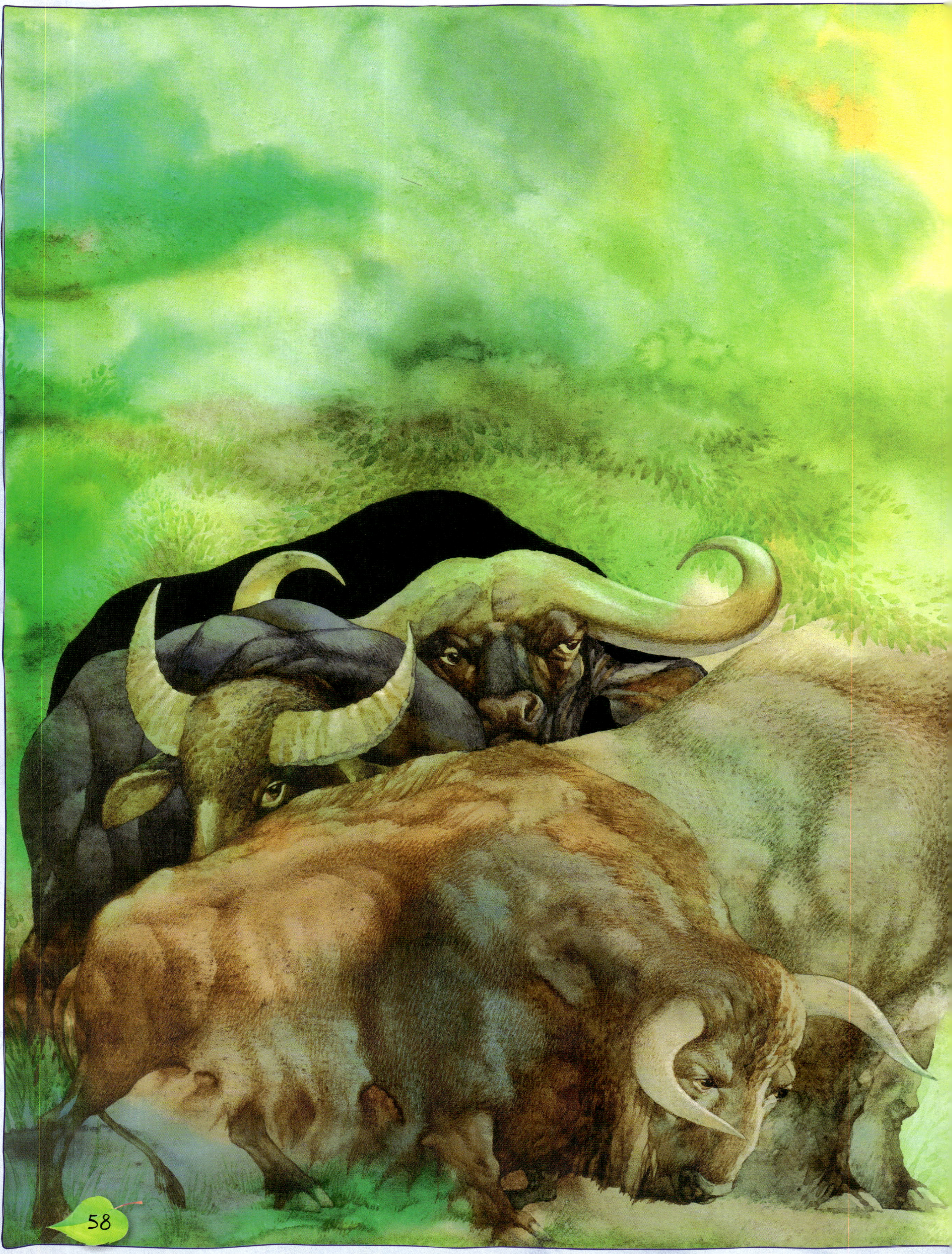

In the great forest there lived four bulls who were truly the best of friends. "We will never separate from one another," they promised each other, "and no animal will ever be able to harm us or trap us."

The four bulls went to graze in the pasture and they were always careful not to leave each other alone. Even the hungry lion who was always looking for a good catch did not dare go near the group of bulls. He looked at the four sets of sharp horns and he understood that he had no chance of trapping any one of the bulls, since they never left each other alone.

One day, when the lion was feeling weak and very hungry, his eyes fell once again on the fat bulls. He waited patiently for an opportunity to catch one of them. Soon, he saw his chance. One of the bulls stepped away from the rest of the group and slowly and peacefully started chewing on some grass.

The lion called out in the direction of the bull in a friendly voice. "My dear beautiful bull, I wish I could be your friend. Let us take a walk together. It will be so much fun. There's no reason to be afraid." With his soft and sweet words, the lion lured the bull to him and, slowly, slowly, drew him away from the rest of the group. That was a big mistake for the bull. Once the bull was all alone, the lion pounced on him and quickly overpowered him. The great bull became a tasty meal for the hungry and clever lion.

What is the lesson?

It is always better to be part of a group than to be alone. When we're together we are protected, but when we separate from the group and go off on our own, we may be heading for trouble.

The Proud Cedar Tree and The Humble Bush

62

In the middle of the forest stood a giant cedar tree, high and mighty above all its surroundings, with a massive trunk and many branches between whose leaves many birds would gather. The cedar tree was very proud, too proud, and in its heart it was sure that it was the king of the forest. It looked to the right, to the left, and then downwards, when suddenly its eyes fell upon a very low-lying bush. It was a thorny bush, very short in height and with very thin branches. It didn't seem to have any important purpose.

"What are you doing here?!" roared the cedar in a very loud voice. "Do you not think it is rude to be growing here pointlessly next to the beautiful and strong cedar tree?!" Without waiting for an answer, it continued proudly, "From my powerful branches they will make axes, pillars and beams, and my tall trunk will one day stand on a ship in the middle of the ocean." Then it started laughing at the thorny bush and said, "And you, what are you?! Is anyone even interested in you?! Will your thin branches succeed at anything?! Ho! Ho! Ha! Ha! Ha! You are completely worthless!!"

Then, suddenly, the bush opened its mouth and it began to answer the proud cedar. "Let your ears hear your very own words, you beautiful and proud cedar. Precisely because you are strong and powerful you will very soon become the victim of a terrible disaster. They will chop you up without any mercy, and then you will no longer tower over all the trees. As for me, whom no one even notices, I will remain right here for many long years after you have been cut down by the lumberjacks. You had better not brag so much, for your end is very near, while my end is nowhere in sight."

What is the lesson?

He who is rich and proud is really not any more secure than his neighbor who is poor and humble.